Lingerie Fantasies

Lingerie Fantasies

Mitchel Gray

St. Martin's Press

New York

I would like to acknowledge the following for their help in making
Lingerie Fantasies a reality:

Authenticolor
Photo Exchange
Photos In-Color
Ford Models
I.M.G. Models
Wilhelmina Models
Zoli Model Management
HV Models
Name Models
Click Models
Harmon-Perella Management
Sehven Arts/August Sehven
Randee-Sue Phillips
Paul Stein
Kalin
Mae Greenwald
Gilbert DeSilva
Juan Gonzalez
Michael Timchula
Oswald "The Gas Station"
Phillip Bleeth Location Vans
Ronald Symth
Ernie Santaniello
David Berg

Lawrine Childers
Joe Hunter
Marian Smith
Deidre D. P. Todaro
Jerry Kaplan
Denise Walch
Jocelyn Braxton
Stephanie Weisman
Michael Landry
Andrew Baseman
Daniela Rondinini
Susan Barr
Rick Teal
Blue Sky Ranch
Frank Traviso
Thierry Van Dieren
Franziska Carrera
Barbara Sansone
Lea van de Donk
Mildred Gray
Winifred Barnes
Jennifer Barnes
Warren Barnes
Mr. & Mrs. Edward Holterhoff

Margie & Allan Synder
Hayley Mortison
Scott Baird
Joel Ely
Ora Feder
The Knole Estate
Esmond B. Martin
Florence Furst
Madison Hardware
Rayelle
Fabio
Cathie Arquilla
Loren Cole
Debbie and Max Lebersfeld
Marjorie Graham
Nancy Menis
Bobby "Big Guy" Fauser
Elaine Good
Wendy Lowy
Kieran Quinn
Ben Slavitt
James Rivera
Bernard Toll Public
 Relations

And my special thanks (above and beyond) to:

Barbara Anderson, editor
Katie Gray, model and stylist
Lisa Meloni, first photo assistant
 and printer

Bruce Strickland, photo assistant
Louis Perella, Perella Management
Art Mszanski, design and layout
Mike Garcia, Authenticolor

Pat Zappel, Authenticolor
Bert Brander, Photo Exchange/
 Photos In-Color
Craig Smyth

And my thanks for spiritual assistance to:

Craig Smyth
Michael Zwack

Richard Liotta
Laverne Washington

Design by Art Mszanski

Library of Congress Cataloging-in-Publication Data
Gray, Mitchel.
Lingerie fantasies / Mitchel Gray.
p. cm.
ISBN 0-312-04149-7
1. Lingerie—Pictorial works. I. Title.
TT670.G74 1990
779'.24'092—dc20 90-37245 CIP

First Edition: September 1990

10 9 8 7 6 5 4 3 2 1

To Katie, for all the help, all the patience,
all the inspiration, and all the love

Introduction

It is now exactly ten years since the publication of *The Lingerie Book*—an appropriate anniversary for assessing the current status of lingerie and its hold over our individual and collective psyches.

In that first book, my goal was to provide a "selected" history of lingerie in the twentieth century, illustrating its evolution from corset to garter belt to bikini—and back again. At the same time I wanted to chronicle the growth of the modern woman from submissive in 1900 to self-assertive in 1990. *The Lingerie Book* was a celebration of women and their unspoken communication with men—and other women—through the medium of lingerie. It was to my great delight that *The Lingerie Book* sold equally well to both men *and* women. The appeal of lingerie is undeniable. It is only one aspect of a woman's dress, but it reaches two of humanity's deepest concerns: our sexuality and our curiosity about the unrevealed. What we don't know has always been far more interesting to us than what we do. As long as these issues remain constant, lingerie will fascinate us.

The last ten years have been a tremendous growth period for lingerie. A great deal of lingerie has been designed as outerwear. Bustiers, camisoles, bejeweled and painted bras, exotic hose, Spandex "exercise" gear, and even G-strings, can be seen readily, anywhere from the street to television to movie theaters to gyms and, of course, on stage at almost any rock concert. These garments go perfectly with the toned, athletic shape of the 1980s and 1990s. They have become an accepted and integral part of our lives.

Given these exciting changes in lingerie, why has it taken me so long to create a second lingerie book? I have been asked this question a thousand times, by everyone from the salespeople at my publisher to my one remote fan in Estonia, USSR. The reason is that I did not want to repeat myself. I wanted a book that would be as fresh and as unique as the first book. I needed a vehicle in which all the forms of lingerie as they exist today could be carried. In searching for this new approach, I kept returning to the notion that women seemed to be drawn to lingerie photographs as strongly as men were. The element of fantasy is such a large part of the appeal of lingerie to both sexes that there had to be a way to harness it for my purposes.

After hours of discussion with Barbara Anderson, my editor at St. Martin's Press, we decided to experiment with a new and unexplored format: We would tell stories with photographs. We would take a single image of a beautiful woman in exquisite lingerie and develop the image into a fantasy—an adult picture story that would lead the "reader" further into his or her own imagination. The stories could be erotic or hard-edged, whimsical or naughty, or purely magic, but each would be a coherent vignette with a "twist" at the end.

With the concept of photo stories, I finally had the vehicle I needed. It would allow me to do two things I love: tell stories and shoot lingerie. I soon found that these lingerie stories—a hybrid form of cinematic "action" and multiple still images—presented many technical difficulties. Finding a balance between memorable imagery and plot advancement was a constant problem. Advancing the storyline too quickly pulled attention away from the images, yet too arresting an image made losing the storyline entirely a distinct possibility. Compromising a potentially alluring photo (in a book of photography) to advance a storyline was unacceptable. Another problem was movement. Simply moving a character from one room to another, so easily accomplished in film because the character can be *seen* moving, can cause the viewer to lose the storyline in this new medium. Lighting techniques and camera angles also had to be adjusted to deal with this new approach. And, lastly, there was the problem of direction. The characters who act out these lingerie fantasies are all models, some of whom, fortunately, had acting experience. However, no one, myself included, had any experience in this new medium. The proper visual and emotional response to situational changes from frame to frame required constant experimentation.

Solutions. First, good plots were essential—ones that were interesting but not so complex that the viewer would get lost. We are all conditioned, by more than one hundred years of still photography, to viewing each frame individually. When the viewer must move from frame to frame to follow a storyline, the photos must flow in terms of action. Any story that is too complex is impossible to follow. Any story without a clever twist at the end is not worth telling or following. Other absolutes were that the stories be sensual and be grounded to some degree in our common experience. Humor proved to be the most universal of all emotions.

The solution to the problem of lighting and camera angles was to take a cinematic path. I would light entire scenes, then modify small areas for cosmetic purposes as the models moved through them. This method of lighting helped in plot perception, because we are used to seeing consistent lighting both in films and in real life. The *suggestion* of place by lighting is usually as effective as seeing the whole place, particularly in closeups. Camera angles were also chosen cinematically.

The solution to the problem of my inexperience in this new medium was to keep direction simple, first explaining the entire story to the models, then describing what actions and reactions were needed as we proceeded through each frame. I left room in my direction for model spontaneity and surprise.

Essential to every shoot for *Lingerie Fantasies* was a well-thought-out storyboard—a frame-by-frame breakdown of who would be in the picture, what they would be doing, and what they would wear. Every film or commercial ever made required a storyboard. They allow everyone involved in the production to know exactly what is expected of them—what locations are needed, what camera and lighting equipment must be used and where it should be placed, what clothing and props are required, and what hair and makeup services will be needed.

The final step in completing each lingerie fantasy was editing and design layout. Because each frame in the book serves two functions—visual pleasure and plot advancement—compromises had to be made at every stage of the edit/design process. Although I did most of the editing, I was often too close to, or too attached to a particular image, to be objective. Both my designer, Art Mszanski, and my editor, Barbara Anderson, were invaluable here. Due to the unique nature of the book, Art Mszanski had no precedents on which to base his work. He spent many long hours sorting through hundreds of photographs and experimenting with various layouts to come up with the right formula that would allow the viewer to perceive both the plot and the beauty within the photograph in the proper proportion.

The creation of *Lingerie Fantasies* presented many unique problems. Finding solutions was both a challenge and an opportunity for technical and artistic growth. I hope that the images and stories presented here will challenge your imagination and that—man or woman—you will enjoy the experience of viewing them, seeing new things, and coming up with your own fantasies each time through.

—MITCHEL GRAY
March 1990

Lipstick

The Lockout

Models: Hayley Mortison, Ford
    Scott Baird (the neighbor), Ford
    Craig Smyth (locksmith)
    Jake the Cat
Stylist: Joel Ely
Hair/Makeup: Lea van de Donk

Sunday
Brunch

Models: Nadja, I.M.G.
    Peter Bordes (boyfriend), Zoli
    Mildred Gray (relative on
    right-hand couch)
    Edward and Helen Holterhoff
    (relatives on left-hand couch)
Stylist: Jocelyn Braxton
Hair/Makeup: Barbara Sansone

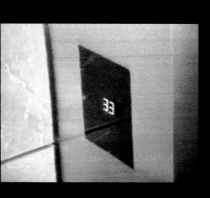

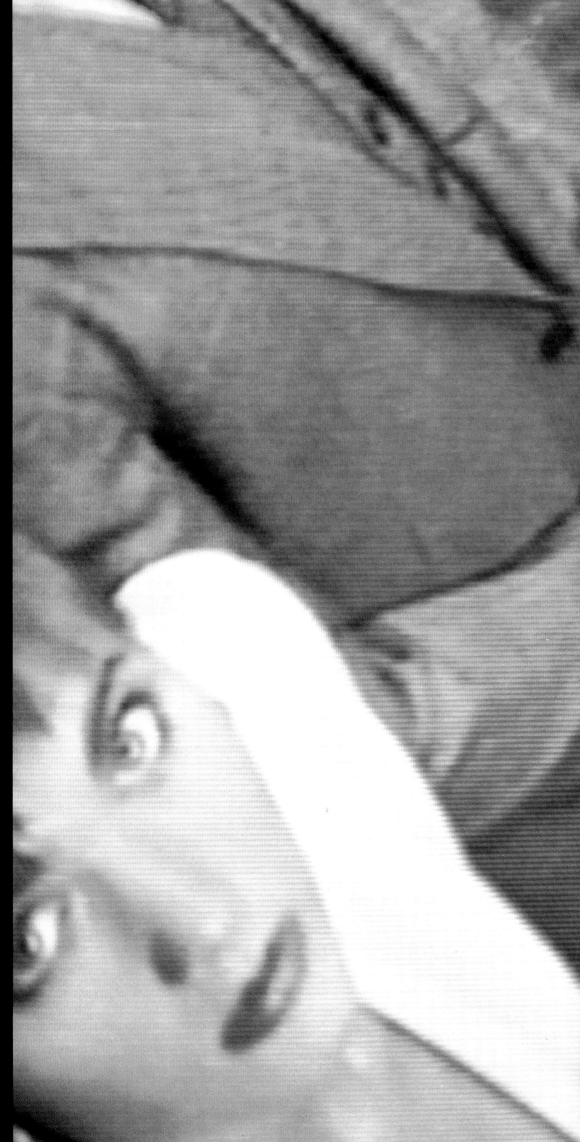

The Elevator

Models: Michelle Boyle, Name
Thom Fleming, Ford Men
David Berg (night watchman)
Stylist: Michael Landry
Hair/Makeup: Rick Teal

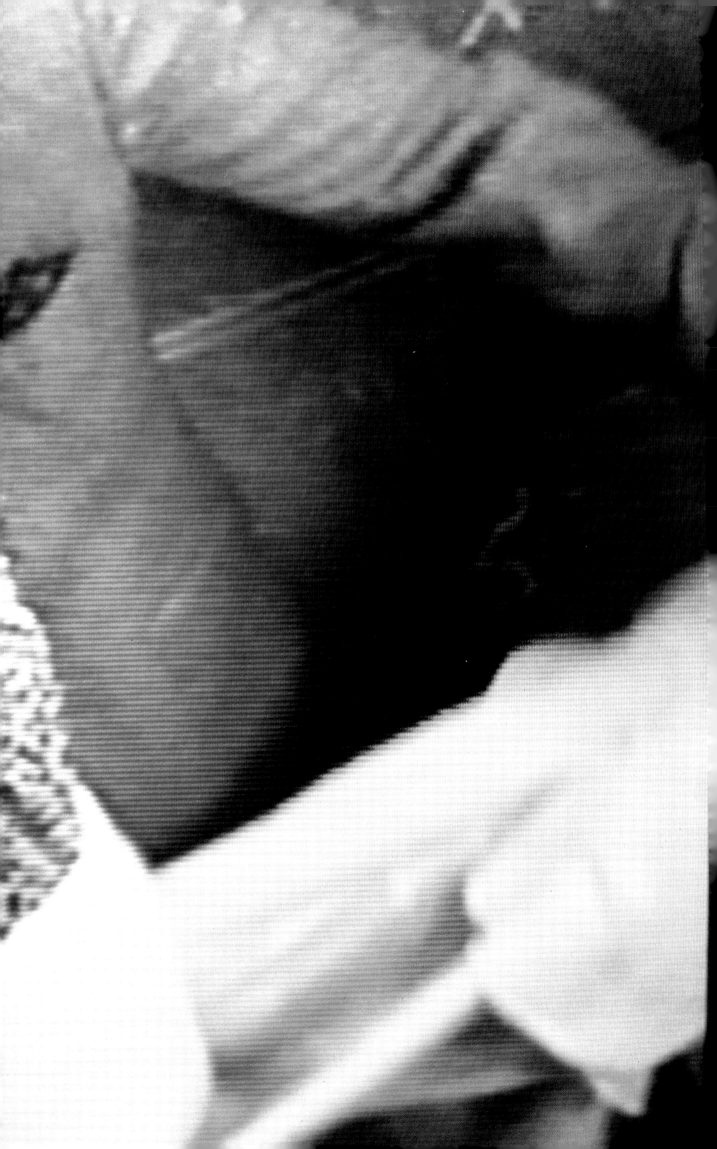

Car & Driver

Models: Hollie Sue, HV
    Luciano, HV
Stylist: Denise Walch
Hair/Makeup: Franziska Carrera

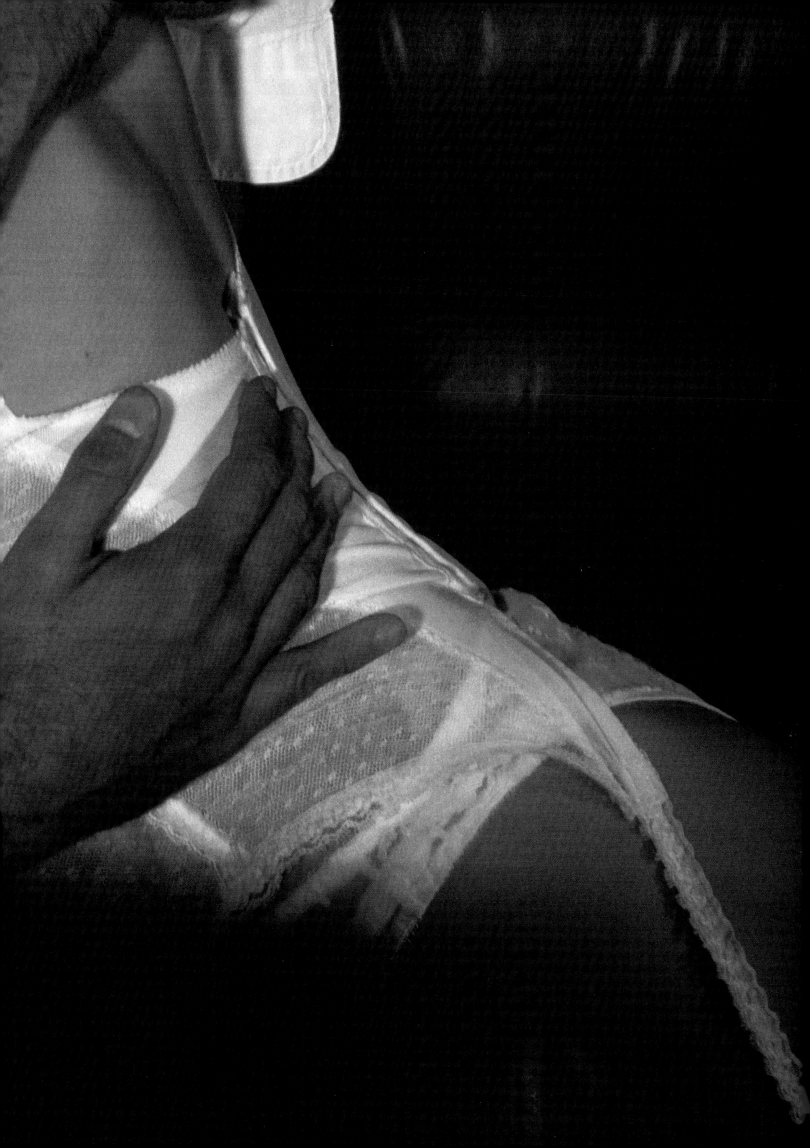

A Formal Affair

Models: Rayelle, HV
Fabio, Ford Men
Stylist: Cathie Arquilla
Hair/Makeup: Loren Cole

Girls' Night Out

Models: Maibritt (woman in
        sunglasses), Ford
        Montana (blond woman in
        dotted stockings), Ford
        Dawn Gallagher (woman in
        earrings and bandana), Ford
        Jennifer Barnes (woman in
        hoop earrings)
        Katie Gray (woman pulling
        scarf)
        Jerry Kaplan (1st cyclist)
        Craig Smyth (2nd cyclist)
        Ernie Santaniello (3rd cyclist)
Stylist: Jocelyn Braxton
Hair/Makeup: Rick Teal
        Thierry Van Dieren

Last Chance

Models: Thom Fleming, Ford Men
Diana Long, Elite
Katie Gray (Bride)
Ben Slavitt (Priest)
Stylist: Cathie Arquilla
Hair/Makeup: Elaine Good

The Bet

Dedicated to Margie and Alan

Model: Tonia, Ford
Stylists: Katie Gray
    "Fred" Barnes
Hair/Makeup: Kathy Gorga

Lingerie Daydreams

#1. Model: Kate Gray
  Stylist: Michael Stein

#2. Model: Kate Gray

#3. Model: Patricia Hamilton,
  Name
  Stylist: Susan Barr
  Hair/Makeup: Lea van de
  Donk

#4. Model: Patricia Hamilton,
  Name
  Stylist: Susan Barr
  Hair/Makeup: Lea van de
  Donk

#5. Model: LaVonne Sherrill

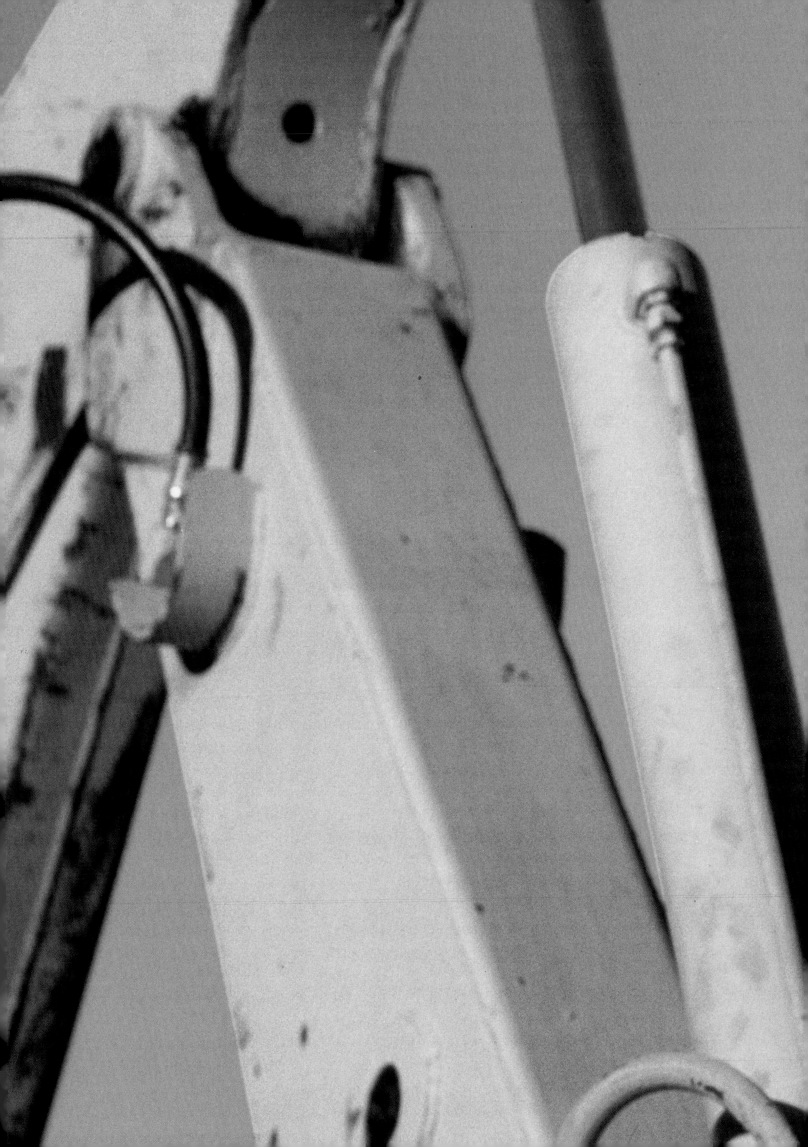

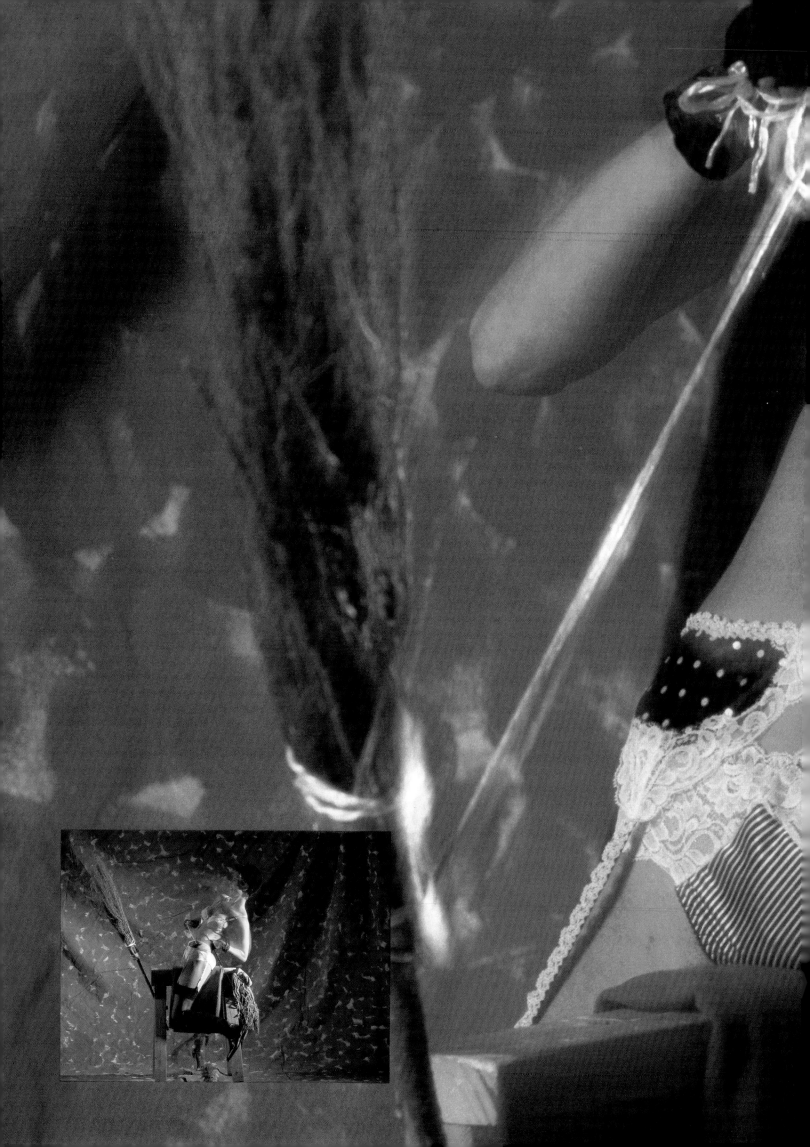

Photo Credits

Cover

Model: Katrina Rae, I.M.G.
Stylist: Andrew Baseman
Hair/Makeup: August Sehven
Resources: Lingerie courtesy of
  Samantha Robbins for Sami Ltd.

Half-Title Page

Model: Nadja, I.M.G.
Stylist: Jocelyn Braxton
Hair/Makeup: Barbara Sansone
Resources: Jeune Europe

Title Page

Model: Terri Corning, Wilhelmina
Stylist: Stephanie Weisman
Hair/Makeup: Rhona Krauss

Lipstick

Model: Kara Myers, Ford

The Lockout

Resources: Ora Feder

Sunday Brunch

Resources: Lingerie: Jeune Europe
  Boyfriend's outfit: Cecelia Metheny
  Shoes: Manolo Blahnik
  Sunglasses: Alain Mikli

The Elevator

Resources: Donna Karan
  Allan Flusser

Car & Driver

Resources: Her suit: Patricia Klein
  Lingerie, Bloomingdale's

A Formal Affair

Resources: Lingerie and sarong: Giorgio
  di Sant'Angelo
  Tuxedo: Pierre Cardin
  Earrings: Eva Kay

Girls' Night Out

Resources: Motorcycles provided by
  Craig Smyth, Randee Sue Phillips,
  Jerry Kaplan, and Ernie Santaniello
Security provided by SafeGuard Security
Location: "The Gas Station" at 2nd
  Street and Avenue B, New York City
Transportation: Phillip Bleeth Location
  Vans
Computerization: Timchula Creative
Lingerie: Piljo, 120 East 7th Street,
  New York City
  Kathrine Love, 64 Avenue A,
  New York City
  Enelra, 48½ East 7th Street,
  New York City
  Hysterics, 93½ East 7th Street,
  New York City
  Untitled, 26 West 8th Street,
  New York City

Scarves and mesh jewelry:
  Island Electric
Additional jewelry: Fragments
Sunglasses: Alain Mikli
Footwear: Maud Frizon

Last Chance

Resources: Location courtesy of Palisades
  Interstate Park Commission—Bear
  Mountain
  Her black garments: all Michelle
  Nicole Wesley except for black thong
  by La Perla.
  Her white lingerie: all La Perla except
  white hose by Michelle Nicole Wesley.
  Formal wear by Lord West.
  Her sunglasses: Christian Lacroix
  His sunglasses: Porsche designed by
  Carrera

The Bet

Resources: Lingerie courtesy of
  "Roberta" of Madison Avenue
Plane and "jump" provided by Blue Sky
  Ranch
Additional photographic assistance:
  Willy Boettcher

Lingerie Daydreams

#2. Resources: Backhoe courtesy of
  Warren Barnes
#3. Resources: Valentino Lingerie
#4. Resources: Robe courtesy of
  Ora Feder
Panties courtesy of Samantha
  Robbins for Sami, Ltd.